Golf Club F Selection for Golfers

Dr. Kurt W. Weingand

Golf Club Fitting and Selection for Amateur Golfers

Copyright © 2022 Dr. Kurt W. Weingand

First Edition

All rights reserved.

ISBN: 9798364509857

DEDICATION

This book is dedicated to amateur golfers around the world. I hope this information helps you understand better the golf club fitting process and your potential selection of new golf clubs. I also hope it enhances your golf performance and your appreciation for this remarkable game and the wonderful fraternity of people that play it world-wide.

ACKNOWLEDGMENTS

I am appreciative to my colleague, Ms. Lori Griffey, a Professional Golfers Association (PGA) professional golfer, and the retired General Manager of the PGA Tour Superstore in North Scottsdale, Arizona. Lori hired me as a part-time golf club fitter. She recognized my talent for fitting golfers with new clubs and delighting them with my service. Lori saw to it that I received the best training available to perfect my skills as a professional golf club fitter. For this, I am very appreciative. Thank you, Lori.

The cover photo is from Kindal Media and was obtained from www.Pexels.com (https://www.pexels.com/photo/golf-balls-and-golf-clubs-in-close-up-photography-6572984/).

This book is not sponsored by any golf companies or brands. Any mentions of golf companies or brands is based solely on my experience with these products.

PREFACE

I've written this book to document my learnings about fitting golfers for golf clubs and selecting new equipment for purchase. These learnings come from five years of working as a certified golf club-fitting professional, several lessons from multiple golf instructors, and my current role as a Clubhouse Coordinator at a public municipal golf course.

This information can be used for training new professional golf club fitters and for amateur golfers that want to learn about the fitting process and gain insights for choosing new golf clubs.

CONTENTS

1	Introduction	1
2	Fitting Irons	6
3	Fitting Drivers	13
4	Fitting Fairway Metals & Hybrids	21
5	Fitting Wedges	22
6	Fitting Putters	25
7	Fitting Golf Balls	28
8	Selecting Irons	30
9	Selecting Drivers	34
10	Selecting Fairway Metals & Hybrids	37
11	Selecting Wedges	38
12	Selecting Putters	41
13	Selecting Shafts	45
14	Selecting Grips	48
15	Selecting Golf Balls	50
16	Selecting Golf Instructors	52
17	Care & Maintenance	54
18	Testimonials	55

1 INTRODUCTION

The game of golf requires expensive equipment (clubs), clothing, and accessories to engage fully. In 2019, global golf club sales were $3.66 billion and were expected to grow 2.5% annually from 2020 to 2027. If you include golf balls, accessories, apparel, and footwear, global golf category sales were $6.85 billion in 2020 and projected to reach $7.6 billion in 2025. Approximately 80% of these sales are purchased by amateur (leisure) golfers (Grand View Research Report ID: GVR-4-68038-809-1, 2019. https://www.grandviewresearch.com/industry-analysis/golf-club-market).

It's challenging for most amateur golfers to play the game well. Playing golf well is a relative concept. Golfers are continually trying to lower their scores and improve their game by getting new and improved equipment and "fiddling" with their golf swing to optimize their ball flight, shot distance, outcomes, and scores. In my experience, well-fitted golf equipment can improve a golfer's performance about 10-15%. Although relatively small, this extent of performance improvement reduces golf scores significantly. Regardless, golfers expect and hope for maximal improvement in their game with new equipment. Original equipment manufacturers (OEMs) leverage this expectation to sell new equipment to golf enthusiasts.

Why is golf so difficult to play well? It's a physical and mental game that requires strength, coordination, balance, and strategic thinking to play well. Patience is very helpful too. Golf is the most challenging problem solving game that I know. It takes time and practice to learn to play the game well.

Golf is more than just a game. In my mind, it is a lifestyle. It's a lifestyle that many golf enthusiasts love. The game is the core attraction, and it entails competitive spirit, camaraderie, and honor. It's a game that can be played by individuals young and old and can be made competitive between golfers of varying capabilities and skills by using the well established handicapping system for play.

I started playing golf in my mid-20's. It was initially an activity to get together with friends and business colleagues outdoors and share a few beers and laughs. My wife, Anne Marie, actually introduced me to the finer points of the game. We started playing golf together when we got married in 1986. It was then that I began my life-long pursuit of golf as a hobby. Thirty-six years have passed, and we still enjoy play golf together regularly across the United States. We enjoy most playing at courses at which we have never played. This variability continually challenges my golf handicap, a 9.9 index in the Golf Handicap Index Network (GHIN). Regardless, we love being outdoors in the fresh air, viewing nature and scenic vistas at beautiful golf courses, and spending time together doing something that we both enjoy.

When I retired from my professional career as a veterinarian, medical scientist, and healthcare product developer, I entered the golf industry as a part-time golf club fitter and salesperson. I began this journey at Golf Galaxy in Cincinnati, Ohio in 2016 and later at the Golf Exchange. Anne Marie and I became "snowbirds" and spent the winter months in Phoenix, Arizona where golf is a big activity for retirees and tourists escaping the cold weather in other regions of the world. In Phoenix, I worked at the PGA Tour Superstore. I became certified as a club fitter by almost all of the OEMs (Titleist, Callaway, TaylorMade, PING, Cobra, Mizuno, Cleveland, Wilson). I also served as a beta-tester of new online training programs for club fitters developed by PING. My background as a data-driven research scientist and consumer products researcher greatly aided my development as a golf club fitting professional and salesperson.

Within the PGA Tour Superstore, I earned national recognition at the annual sales meeting in 2018 as an employee that exemplified one of the company's core values, Giving Back to Others. I became a specialist at club fitting and trained new employees on the company process and our approach to sales. Using a low-pressure, data-based approach, I was able to successfully fit hundreds of golfers with new clubs and delight them with improved performance and outcomes. Testimonials from some of my customers are provided in a chapter later in this book.

Club fitting is a professional service that can be obtained at national big-box golf specialty retail stores (PGA Tour Superstore, Golf

Galaxy), small regional golf specialty stores (Golf Exchange, Vans Golf Shops), boutique golf specialty stores that focus on building custom fit clubs (True Spec, Club Champion, GolfTec, Cool Clubs, Hot Stix), many local golf courses by club pros, green-grass (golf course) club fitting events sponsored by OEMs, OEM specific retail outlets (PXG), or at private OEM fitting facilities (PING).

Most of these providers charge for golf club fitting services, and cost can range from $50 to $500 based on the time and technical methods used to conduct the fitting. If a club is purchased, the fitting fee is sometimes deducted (comped) from the cost of the clubs.

The PGA Tour Superstore is unique in that they offer complimentary club fitting services to their customers. This is either a 20-30 minute session for fitting irons, a similar session for fitting a driver, or both. This free fitting service is sufficient to properly fit and equip most amateur golfers. More comprehensive and technical club fitting is also available for a service fee in the PGA Tour Superstore Fitting Studios (previously called PGA Tour Superstore Fitting Vans) with availability to test unique custom (after-market) golf club shaft offerings that are not offered by the OEMs.

I mainly did routine complimentary club fittings, but I was also trained by master club fitters to work in the PGA Tour Superstore Fitting Van. As a part-time worker, my time working in the Fitting Van was limited. I am appreciative to have worked with two highly talented professional golfers, Messrs. Bill Kuikman and Andrew Silverman, and a master fitter, Mr. Joe Pike, who collectively taught me a great deal about fitting golfers for new clubs, optimizing golfer set-up at address, ball striking, and ball flight dynamics.

For clarity, I am a certified golf professional, not a professional golfer. I was not trained to teach golfers how to swing a golf club and play golf. Golf instruction is the job of Professional Golfers Association (PGA) certified professional golfers. I worked collaboratively with several excellent PGA certified instructors at the PGA Tour Superstore. If a potential golf club customer did not have the skills to simply hit a golf ball, I would send them to one of our PGA instructors to develop their skills before purchasing new clubs. This led to better and happier golf customers and fewer returns on purchases of new clubs through the company's 90 Day Performance Guarantee program. It was a win-win-win approach for our golf customers, our instructors, and company business performance.

Although I'm not a PGA certified golf instructor, I have developed significant skill in helping golfers improve their set-up (grip, posture, stance, and ball selection) to optimize their results in trying new clubs for potential purchase. I told people that I was fitting them with golf clubs for the swing that they currently have. If they did not perform well on the day of the fitting, I recommended that they come back another day when they were physically and mentally fresh. I also recommend that customers get fitted for irons in a separate fitting session from the driver and fairway metals. Golfers simply get tired after making about 50 swings comparing their current clubs to 3 or 4 new clubs during a 20-30 minute fitting session.

To my knowledge, the PGA certification training program contains minimal information about golf club fitting. As such, many PGA professional golfers at golf clubs in Phoenix would send their clients to me to get a complimentary fitting at the PGA Tour Superstore. They knew that we did an excellent job and trusted our fitting recommendations. It was then up to the client to decide where to purchase their new clubs. I gave the golfer a written fitting recommendation with club set specifications and a price quote for the recommended clubs for purchase. It's hard to find a better opportunity (complimentary fitting) and competitive price for new golf clubs for an amateur golfer than what is offered at some golf specialty retail stores.

The club fitting professional is a key influencer in the selection of golf clubs by golfers. The fitter commonly initiates a relationship with the potential customer at the retail store product shelf (the "first moment of truth"). The fitter then has the opportunity to recommend specific models of clubs for the golfer to try and compare to their current clubs, (the "second moment of truth"). The club fitter is in a very influential position for the purchase of new golf clubs. The potential customer usually buys one of the golf club models that they touch, feel, and try by hitting golf balls, not the ones that they don't.

With the advent of the global corona virus pandemic of 2019, virtual (video) club "fittings" became popular. Virtual fittings in the absence of actually swinging and feeling specific clubs, hitting balls, and seeing shot outcomes, is simply a method of consultation for purchase of new golf clubs. It's better than nothing, but a true hands-on club fitting experience with demonstrable objective measures of shot performance is superior to a virtual consultation in my mind.

Legendary golf instructor, John Jacobs, has been credited for saying, "Golf is what the ball does. The effect we create on the golf ball is the only absolute in the game. How a player specifically does it, is another question."

In my opinion, golf equipment and technology can significantly improve golf shot performance, but talent, skill, physical ability, and strategic thinking are most important for playing the game of golf well.

In this book I provide key insights for fitting amateur golfers for the selection and purchase of new golf clubs including the driver, fairway metals, hybrids, irons, wedges, and a putter. I also discuss the selection of shafts and balls to optimize golfer performance. In addition, I share my experiences and recommendations for golf instruction by certified PGA professional golfers. I also provide some tips for care and maintenance of golf equipment.

2 FITTING IRONS

The golf club fitting process for irons should be done methodically in the following order.

1. Conduct a pre-fit interview with the golfer to define needs and desired outcomes from new clubs.
2. Determine the optimum golf club head model.
3. Determine the optimum shaft length and flex.
4. Determine the optimum club head loft and lie angle.
5. Optimize the shot shape desired.
6. Fine tune the shaft for desired performance outcomes.
7. Determine the optimum golf grip.

The main goal for most amateur golfers with moderate to low swing speeds is to get the lightest (lowest weight) golf club (head and shaft) that the golfer can swing fast to maximize shot distance without losing shot accuracy. In contrast, better players with fast swing speeds usually benefit from a relatively heavy golf club weight.

The process starts with a golfer interview and discussion of golfer needs and desires for the purchase of new clubs. How long have you played golf? Do you have an established handicap? What is your average score for an 18 hole round of golf? How far do you hit your current driver? If you want to hit a 150 yard shot, what club do your use? What is your most common shot shape when you strike the ball well, i.e., straight, draw (right-to-left for right handed golfer) or fade (left-to-right for right handed golfer)? When you hit a bad shot off the target line, do miss right or left most often? Do you create a divot in the grass with your current irons? How big are your divots with your iron shots? If you could improve either shot distance or accuracy, which one do you desire most from new irons? What kind of irons to you have now? Do you have your current irons with you for comparison to new ones? What's most important to you, iron performance or appearance? Do you have any specific brands or models of irons that you want to try? What kind of golf ball do your currently use when playing golf? What is the maximum price that you want to invest in new irons?

The answer to the question about which club is used to hit a 150 yard shot can give the fitter some general subjective insight into the flex of shaft that may be optimal. The relationship of approximate shaft flex to the club used to hit a 150 yard shot is shown in Table 1. This information gives the fitter a general idea of what shaft flexes to start testing and can be augmented objectively by measuring ball speed during the warm-up process with the golfer's current club.

TABLE 1: Shaft Flex for 150 Yard Shot

Shaft Flex	Iron
Extra Stiff (X, F5*, 6.5-7.5**)	9 iron
Stiff (S, F4, 5.5-6.4)	8 iron
Regular (R, F3, 4.5-5.4)	7 iron
Senior or Mature or Amateur (S, M, A, SR***, F2, R2, 3.5-4.4)	6 iron
Ladies (L, F1, R3, 2.5-3.4)	5 iron
Ladies Light or Junior (LL, F0, JR)	4 hybrid

*UST, Fujikura, Aerotech
**Project X frequency coefficients
***PING Soft Regular

With answers to the golfer interview questions, I choose 3 to 4 new club types for the golfer to try and compare to their current club. This process will be discussed further in the chapter on Selecting Irons.

As for specific brands and models of golf clubs, all of the OEMs make excellent quality golf clubs. Each have models for experienced better players with advanced skills, good golfers that aspire to improve their game, and beginners that need help getting the golf ball in the air and flying relatively straight to maximize game enjoyment.

Most golf club irons provided by OEMs for demonstration (demo) purposes are 7 (or 6) irons. Demo drivers, fairway woods, hybrids, and wedges are also provided by the OEMs. If the golfer used a specific golf ball, I use that specific brand and model for the fitting process. Using relatively new golf balls in the fitting process is especially important for fitting wedges where backspin data is most meaningful for stopping power and the desired outcome.

I start the fitting process with the golfer's current 7 iron with a piece of face tape on the club. I ask the golfer to step into the golf simulator hitting bay and take 8-10 shots to get warmed up. I take the face tape off of the club face after the first 4-5 shots, as it can decrease backspin on the ball with iron shots. I record these warm up shots with the simulator program and keep the best 4 or 5 shots as the data representing their optimum performance capability with their current club. The key measurements for comparison are distance (carry and total) and accuracy (dispersion). Many other variables are measured including ball speed, back spin, and launch angle. From the ball speed data, I can estimate the club head speed which is approximately 2/3 (66%) of the ball speed on good solid shots. Ball speed is most important, as it includes assessment of ball striking quality resulting from the club head speed delivered at impact.

I take biometric or "static" fitting measurements of the golfers body height with their golf shoes on and then the wrist-to-floor distance of the golf glove (non-dominant) hand. Some of the OEMs provide tables for estimating the length and lie angle of demo clubs to begin the "dynamic" (ball striking) fitting process.

I analyze the club impact position on the face tape from the golfers current club. If the impact marks are consistent and precise near the center of the club face, the shaft length is optimal. If the impact marks are variable, a shorter club length and/or an adjustment in the golfer's posture or distance from the ball at setup should be considered. An assessment of shaft length should be done before measuring the lie angle, because the club length can significantly affect the dynamic lie angle measurements.

I start the new club testing process with the shaft flex associated with the golfer's ball speed recorded during their best warm-up swings with their current club. The optimum shaft flex for golf ball and club head speeds is shown in Table 2. This is simply a guideline for new club testing. The optimum shaft flex will ultimately be determined by ball flight outcomes (distance and dispersion), swing tempo, and feel by the golfer.

TABLE 2: Optimum Iron Shaft Flex for Ball and Club Head Speed

Shaft Flex	Ball Speed (mph)	Club Head Speed (mph)
Extra Stiff (X, F5*, 6.5-7.5**)	135-150	90-100
Stiff (S, F4, 5.5-6.4)	120-135	80-90
Regular (R, F3, 4.5-5.4)	105-120	70-80
Senior/Mature/Amateur (S, M, A, SR***, F2, R2, 3.5-4.4)	90-105	60-70
Ladies (L, F1, R3, 2.5-3.4)	75-90	50-60
Ladies Light or Junior (LL, F0, JR)	<75	<50

*UST, Fujikura, Aerotech
**Project X frequency coefficients
***PING Soft Regular

<u>The golfer's swing tempo significantly influences the determination of the optimum shaft flex</u>. Golfers with a fast tempo may benefit from a stiffer flex, while golfers with a slow tempo may benefit from a more flexible shaft.

I do not tell the golfer what shaft flex they're hitting with the demo irons, as it biases their qualitative assessment of the club. When a golfer asks what the flex was of the shaft that he/she was hitting, I simply say, "I'll share all information about the test clubs when we're done hitting balls." Shaft selection is determined both qualitatively by golfer feel and the quantitative outcomes. Golf shaft selection will be discussed further in detail in the chapter Selecting Shafts.

From the answers to the interview questions and the information gained watching the golfer hitting their current 7 iron, I choose 3-4 demo irons for the golfer to try. I will provide key insights on this important choice in the chapter on Selecting Irons.

For each demo iron tested, I ask the golfer to hit 6 shots. I take the best 4 shots and use this data for comparison to their current club. The data generated is usually very revealing. One or two of the new clubs tested usually perform better than their current club. I then ask them to hit the best two performing demo clubs again. This time, I ask the golfer to focus on the qualitative feel of the club. I would record another 4 or 5 shots with the top performing clubs and add that data to the existing database. Ideally, one club model stands out as better for distance and/or accuracy when compared to their current club. If there is no demonstrable improvement in performance with the new irons, then there is no objective reason to purchase new irons.

If there is an objective demonstrable improvement in distance or accuracy, I then measure and confirm of the optimal lie angle of the superior club. There are several ways to do this, but I like assessing the lie angle by putting a piece of face tape on the club and recording the dynamic angle of ball impact on the club face. This is done by drawing a straight thin line about 1 inch long on the golf ball with a dry-erase marker. Dry-erase markers do not stain the white hitting screens in the simulator like a permanent ink (Sharpie®) marker can. After marking the ball with the dry-erase marker, the ball is placed with the marked line straight vertical facing opposite of the target line, i.e., the side of the ball that the golfer will strike with the club. The player then strikes the ball, and an imprint of the marker line from the ball is left on the club face tape. By analyzing the angle of the ink strike mark on the club face relative to the horizontal sole of the club, one can see the exact lie angle of the club at the moment of impact. If the face tape line is perpendicular to the sole of the club, the club lie angle is optimal. If the top of face tape line is angled toward the heel of the club with a right-handed golfer, the lie angle is too flat (toe down at impact), and a more upright (larger) lie angle should be tested (see illustration below). This iron face tape is from a fitting with a right-handed golfer. The ball impact mark is on the toe of the club, but the top of the big dark impact line imprinted from the ball angles toward the heel 1 degree.

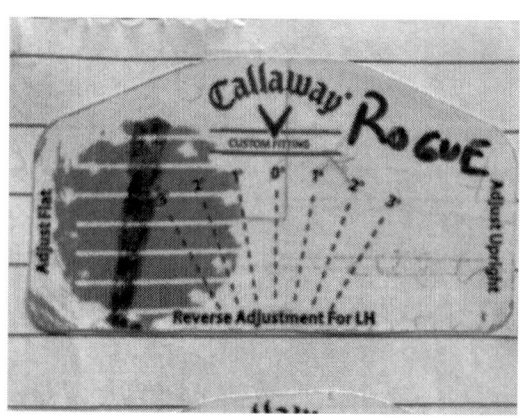

If the top of face tape line is angled toward the toe of the club with a right-handed golfer, the lie angle is too upright (toe up at impact), and a flatter (smaller) lie angle should be tested. This is an iterative process that I have found to be the most simple and accurate way to find the ideal lie angle. In general, taller (>6 ft) people may perform better with longer shafts and more upright (larger) lie angles. Shorter people (<5 feet 7 inches) may do better with shorter shafts and flatter (smaller) lie angles. It really depends on how long the golfers arms are relative to their height.

This diagnostic lie angle data is very useful, but the ultimate factor in determining the best club fit is the ball flight outcome. The ball flight outcomes alway supersede any diagnostic data. When the ball flight is straight, that is the golfer's optimum lie angle regardless of the diagnostic face tape recordings. If the measured diagnostic data does not optimize ball flight data, PING recommends using the club length and lie angle recommendations in the their static fitting chart. In my experience, the PING fitting chart is highly predictive of the optimum iron fit for amateur golfers (see https://ping.com/en-us/fitting/our-process/irons).

The lie angle can also be measured with club sole tape, a digital gyroscope in a specialized fitting shaft (Mizuno), or with a specialized photoelectric methods, but in my experience, the face tape method is simple, accurate, and sufficient for fitting most amateur golfers with irons.

If a golfer needs a specific lie angle other than standard, I recommend special ordering the irons directly from the manufacturer to assure validity of the purchase warranty. Some OEMs will not honor a purchase warranty if the clubs have been bent to adjust the lie angle after purchase.

As a final step, fine tuning the iron shaft selection for amateur golfers is done by trying a shaft that is 10 grams (g) lighter in weight to see if ball speed and distance can be improved without decreasing accuracy (increasing shot dispersion). For better players, an iron shaft that is 10 g heavier in weight can be tried. The final shaft selection is highly subjective and determined by both objective data and feel to the golfer.

I do not recommend stiff or soft-stepping iron shafts to alter the flex. Stepping is a club building method in which you install a different iron shaft than specifically designed for an iron club head, e.g., placing an 8 iron shaft in a 7 iron club head (stiff or hard step) or a 6 iron shaft in a 7 iron club head (soft step). A single step hard or soft only changes the flex about 25%. Most important, the golfer cannot demo a stepped club until it is manufactured.

After the optimum club head, lie angle, and shaft have been identified, the optimum grip size should be chosen. Grip texture and size a re personal preferences of the golfer for comfort. Hand charts are available at most fitting facilities to measure the length of the hands and fingers as a guideline for choosing grip size. Qualitatively, when gripping the club with the left hand (right handed golfer), the last two fingers (pinky and ring finger) should wrap around the end portion of the grip and barely touch the fleshy part of the palm of the hand. Golf Pride has an online guide for measurement of grip size (see https://www.golfpride.com/fit/).

Grips come in standard, midsize, jumbo, ladies, and extra-small (kids) sizes. Most demo clubs for fitting have standard rubber grips. The most important factor in choosing grips is the weight of the grip. Standard rubber grips weigh approximately 50 grams. Rubber is a dense material and can add significant weight to a club with addition of a rubber mid-size or jumbo grip. Mid-size rubber grips can weigh up to 65 grams. Addition of significant weight to the grip end of the club can decrease swingweight, feel for the club head, and shot performance resulting in fades or slices for a right handed golfer (see https://ping.com/en-us/blogs/proving-grounds/get-a-grip). If you prefer mid-size or jumbo grips, choose a model made of relatively light weight material. Synthetic polymer grip materials are lighter and a better option when choosing large (mid-size or jumbo) grip sizes. Mid-size Winn Dri-Tac grips are equivalent in weight to standard rubber grips.

3 FITTING DRIVERS

I recommend fitting the driver in a separate fitting session from the irons. Golfers get tired after an iron fitting session and run out of energy and concentration for fitting additional clubs.

The OEMs provide a wide variety of demo drivers for fitting purposes. The driver is the second most important golf club (putter is first), and the one that amateur golfers are most interested in trying to attain longer shot distance and accuracy.

The fitting process for drivers should be done methodically in the following order.

1. Conduct a pre-fit interview with the golfer to define needs and desired outcomes from a new driver.
2. Determine the optimum golf club head model.
3. Determine the optimum shaft length and flex.
4. Determine the optimum club head loft.
5. Optimize the shot shape desired.
6. Fine tune the shaft for desired performance outcomes.
7. Determine the optimum golf grip.

The main goal for most amateur golfers with moderate to low driver club head swing speeds (<90 mph) is to get the lightest golf club (total head, shaft, and grip weight) that the golfer can swing fast to maximize shot distance without losing shot accuracy. Better players may benefit from a heavier total golf club weight.

The process starts with the golfer interview and discussion of golfer needs and desires for the purchase of a driver. How long have you played golf? Do you have an established handicap? What is your average score for an 18 hole round of golf? How far do you hit your current driver when playing golf? What is your most common shot shape when you strike the ball well, i.e., straight, draw (right-to-left for right handed golfer) or fade (left-to-right for right handed golfer)? When you hit a bad shot off the target line, do miss the fairway right or left most often? Do break your tees often when you hit your current driver? If you could improve either shot distance or accuracy, which one would you desire most from a new driver? What kind of driver do you use now? Do you have your current driver with you for comparison to a new one? What's most important to you, driver performance or appearance? Do you have any specific brands or models of drivers that you want to try? What kind of golf ball do you use? What is the maximum price that you want to invest in a new driver?

The answer to the question about how far the golfer hits their drive when playing golf is tricky. The reality is that most amateur golfs do not know how far they hit their driver, and they commonly overestimate this distance significantly. Golfers are commonly disappointed in the distance that they hit their driver using an indoor golf simulator and frequently question the accuracy of the method used for measurement. As long as I use the same method to quantitate outcomes on both the golfer's current club and the new demo clubs, the comparison is accurate and relevant for measuring differences between drivers and making a data-based decision for purchasing new clubs.

I start the new driver testing process with the shaft flex associated with the golfer's ball speed recorded during their best 4-6 warm-up swings with their current club. The optimum shaft flex for golf ball and driver club head speeds is shown in Table 3. This is simply a guideline for new club testing, not a rigid, inflexible standard. The optimum shaft flex will ultimately be determined by ball flight outcomes (distance and dispersion), swing tempo, and feel to the golfer.

<u>The golfer's swing tempo significantly influences the determination of the optimum shaft flex</u>. Golfers with a fast tempo may benefit from a stiffer flex, while golfers with a slow tempo may benefit from a more flexible shaft.

TABLE 3: Optimum Driver Shaft Flex for Ball and Club Head Speed

Shaft Flex	Ball Speed (mph)	Club Head Speed (mph)
Extra Stiff (X, F5*, 6.5-7.5**)	>165	>110
Stiff (S, F4, or 5.5-6.4)	135-165	90-110
Regular (R, F3, 4.5-5.4)	120-135	80-90
Senior/Mature/Amateur (S, M, A, SR***, F2, R2, 3.5-4.4)	105-120	70-80
Ladies (L, F1, R3, 2.5-3.4)	90-105	60-70
Ladies Light or Junior (LL, F0, JR)	<90	<60

*UST, Fujikura, Aerotech
**Project X frequency coefficients
***PING Soft Regular

I do not tell the golfer what shaft flex they're hitting with the demo drivers, as it biases their qualitative assessment of the club. When a golfer asks what the flex was of the shaft that he/she was hitting, I simply say, "I'll share all information about the test clubs when we're done hitting balls." Shaft selection is determined both qualitatively by golfer feel and the quantitative outcomes. Golf shaft selection will be discussed further in detail in the chapter Selecting a Shaft.

I start the fitting process with the golfer's current driver with a piece of face tape on the club face to develop a face map of ball impact marks. If the golfer uses a specific golf ball to play golf, I use that specific brand and model for the fitting process. I ask the golfer to step into the golf simulator hitting bay and take 8-10 shots to get warmed up. Face tape does not significantly affect diagnostic data measured with the driver. I record these warm up shots with the simulator program and keep the best 4 or 5 shots as the data representing their optimum performance capability with their current driver. The key measurements for comparison are distance (carry and total) and accuracy (dispersion). Many other diagnostic data variables are measured including ball speed, back spin, and launch angle. From the ball speed data, I can estimate the driver club head speed which is approximately 2/3 (66%) of the ball speed on good solid shots. Ball speed is most important, as it includes assessment of ball striking quality resulting from the club head speed delivered at impact.

The fitter needs to know if their simulator method makes direct measurements of ball speed, club head speed, or both. Methods that measure only one variable commonly calculate an estimate of the other. That's reasonable, but I think using a calculated estimate in either ball or club head speed to calculate another variable (smash factor) is dubious. Smash factor is the calculated ratio of ball speed divided by club head speed. Theoretically, a smash factor for a ball hit perfectly in the center of the face of a driver is 1.5 (1.37 for irons). My issue with using smash factor for evaluation of the quality (centered) face impacts is that this calculated estimate is eventually related directly to only one direct measurement of either ball speed or club head speed. As such, smash factor is superfluous data point in my mind, so I rely most on the one variable measured directly. If both ball speed and club head speed are measure directly, then calculation of the smash fact is somewhat meaningful. The issue is that true club head speed is difficult to measure, as the toe, center face, and heel all move at different rates during a swing (see https://ping.com/en-us/blogs/proving-grounds/smashing-smash-factor). With the simulators I have used, ball speed was the direct measurement and reflected indirectly the outcome of both the speed of the club and the resultant quality of the impact on the face. I rely on face mapping the club face with face tape, to assess the quality of golf ball impact with the club face. PING recommends using ball speed for evaluation of driver performance.

From the answers to the interview questions and the information gained watching the golfer hitting their current driver, I choose 3-4 drivers for the golfer to try. I will provide key insights on this important choice in the chapter on Selecting Drivers.

For each demo driver tested, I ask the golfer to hit 6 shots with face tape on the driver. I take the best 4 shots and use this data for comparison to their current driver. One or two of the new drivers tested usually perform better than their current club. I then ask them to hit the best two performing demo drivers again. This time, I ask the golfer to focus on the quality and feel of the club. I record another 4 or 5 shots with the top performing drivers and add that data to the existing database. Ideally, one driver model stands out as better for distance and/or accuracy when compared to their current driver. If there is no demonstrable objective improvement in performance with the new driver, there is no reason to purchase a new club.

How do you optimize performance of new drivers? The simplest way to improve driver shot distance and accuracy is to hit the ball in the center of the club face. That's easier said than done. Many of the new drivers on the market have shafts that are simply too long for amateur golfers to control and hit the ball with precision. If the face map of impact marks on the driver club face are highly variable, shortening the shaft may be an opportunity for performance improvement.

To explore shaft length as a variable, I take a piece of brightly colored tape, 1 inch wide, and wrap it around the very end of the driver grip. I tell the golfer that the edge of the tape closest to the club head is now the new imaginary end of the club and to grip down on the shaft appropriately. I put a new piece of face tape on the driver and have the golfer hit 4-6 shots. If the face map impact pattern with the "shorter shaft" is more consistent and precise in the center of the club, I recommend shortening the shaft length, i.e., trimming the butt end of the shaft by 1 inch, for purchase of a new driver. If the face map impacts are still variable and imprecise, add another 0.5 to 1 inch piece of tape to create and new imaginary end of the club and have the golf hit another 4-6 shots on a new piece of face tape. I always ask the golfer how the club feels while hitting balls with a shorter shaft grip. Ideally, the quantitative (face map) and qualitative (feel) assessments will agree. If the driver shaft needs to be shortened, I recommend butt trimming the grip end to attain the desired length, because tip trimming also increases stiffness of the shaft.

Innovation in driver technology has produced models with fixed and adjustable loft, face angle, center-of-gravity (COG), and lie angle. These drivers can be adjusted manually to modify golf ball launch angle and backspin to optimize ball carry distance, roll out, trajectory and shot shape.

The goal for most amateur golfers with moderate swing speeds (80-90 mph) is to maximum distance and accuracy by getting center hits on the club face with a ball launch angle of 12-15 degrees and 2,000-2,500 rpm of backspin. For better players with fast driver club head speeds (>90 mph), they gain better driver performance by hitting low trajectory drives that roll out maximally on the fairway. Better players with fast swing speeds strive for ball launch angles of 9-12 degrees with 1,750-2,250 rpm of backspin. Players with slow driver club head speeds (<80 mph) can maximize driver performance by maximizing ball flight carry in the air with ball launch angles of 15-20 degrees and backspins in the range of 2,500-3,000 rpm to maximize shot trajectory height. These data are summarized in Table 4.

TABLE 4: Optimizing Driver Diagnostic Data

Club Head Speed (mph)	Launch Angle (degrees)	Backspin (rpm)
>90	9-12	1,750-2,250
80-90	12-15	2,000-2,500
<80	15-20	2,500-3,000

The reality is that strong, flexible, young players can swing their golf clubs faster than less flexible, older players. The amount of ball backspin should be minimized for golfers with high swing speeds to maximize roll out on the fairway and maximized for moderate to low swing speeds to increase the height of ball flight trajectory and carry distance.

Accuracy and distance can also be improved for the driver by adjusting the loft angle. A good starting point for fitting amateur golfers with a driver is 10.5 degrees of loft. The hosel shaft adapter can be adjusted during the fitting to test lower or higher lofts with the same club. For most drivers, adjustments to increase the loft also close the club face angle, while adjustments to decrease the loft open the club face angle. If these loft adjustments cause increased shot dispersion (decreased accuracy) or alteration of the desired shot pattern because of changes in the face angle, the fitter should consider testing a driver with pre-fixed lower (9-10 degrees) or higher (11-12 degrees) lofts. With a fixed driver loft by design, the driver face angle is not altered and should be delivered square at ball impact as designed.

Accuracy can also be improved with driver designs that vary the COG and/or club head offset (distance between the leading edge of the shaft and the leading edge of the club face) to delay the time before impact and allow for increased closing of the club face angle. Drivers with increased offset are useful for minimizing a fade or slice and maximizing a draw shot pattern. Placing the COG toward the toe minimizes "gear effect" on toe hits that may cause excessive draw or a hooking shot pattern while placing the COG toward the heel of the driver minimizes potential gear effect that may cause excessive fades or slices. Gear effect is the sidespin created when the COG of the club head and ball are not aligned, creating a "COG-offset" that causes twisting of the club face and results in increased sidespin of the ball. Of interest, gear effects do not occur when striking irons.

Driver designs that put the COG toward the back of the driver increase ball backspin, while designs that put the COG toward the front of the driver decrease ball backspin. Driver designs that put the COG high in the club head decrease ball launch angle, while designs that put the COG low in the club head increase ball launch angle. All of these driver designs and adjustments can be considered and tried in a fitting session with golfers considering the purchase of a new driver.

Fine tuning the shaft selection for amateur golfers (especially those with moderate to low swing speeds) can be done by trying a shaft that is 10 grams (g) lighter in weight to see if ball speed and distance can be improved without decreasing accuracy (increasing shot dispersion). For better players with fast swing speeds, a shaft that is 10 g heavier in weight can be tried for the same purpose. The final shaft selection is determined primarily the subjective feel to the golfer and will be discussed in detail in the chapter on Selecting Shafts.

If shortening of the shaft is indicated, this can decrease the objective swingweight and decrease the subjective feel for the club head (too light) during a swing. If shortening the shaft length alters the golfer's swing dynamics and perception of swing quality, the swingweight can be increased on a shorter club by using a heavier weight class shaft or by increasing the weight of the shortened shaft by placing lead tape on the distal (club) end of the shaft 1-4 inches above the shaft adapter to optimize the qualitative feel while swinging the club. I do not put lead tape on the club head, because it can alter the center-of-gravity (COG) of the club head resulting in changes in the ball launch angle and backspin depending on where the lead tape is placed on the club head. Alternatively, if the golfer prefers not to shorten (trim) the shaft, a variable face-map impact pattern can also be improved by counter-balancing the butt end of the shaft by using a heavy rubber grip. For the record, I have never added lead tape to a golf club shaft to optimize a club fitting for an amateur golfer. I have successfully recommended heavier grips to counter-balance a club to improve swing feel.

After the optimum club head, lie angle, and shaft have been identified, the optimum grip size should be chosen. Grip texture and size a re personal preferences of the golfer for comfort. Hand charts are available at most fitting facilities to measure the length of the hands and fingers as a guideline for choosing grip size. Qualitatively, when gripping the club with the left hand (right handed golfer), the last two fingers (pinky and ring finger) should wrap around the end portion of the grip and barely touch the fleshy part of the palm of the hand. Golf Pride has an online guide for measurement of grip size (see https://www.golfpride.com/fit/).

Grips come in standard, midsize, jumbo, ladies, and extra-small (kids) sizes. Most demo clubs for fitting have standard rubber grips. The most important factor in choosing grips is the weight of the grip. Standard rubber grips weigh approximately 50 grams. Rubber is a dense material and can add significant weight to a club with addition of a rubber mid-size or jumbo grip. Mid-size rubber grips can weigh up to 65 grams. Addition of significant weight to the grip end of the club can decrease swingweight, feel for the club head, and shot performance resulting in fades or slices for a right handed golfer (see https://ping.com/en-us/blogs/proving-grounds/get-a-grip). If you prefer mid-size or jumbo grips, choose a model made of relatively light weight material. Synthetic polymer grip materials are lighter and a better option when choosing large (mid-size or jumbo) grip sizes. Mid-size Winn Dri-Tac grips are equivalent in weight to standard rubber grips.

4 FITTING FOR FAIRWAY METALS AND HYBRIDS

I recommend fitting of fairway metals and hybrids in a separate fitting session from the driver or irons. Golfers get tired after a driver or iron fitting session and run out of energy and concentration for fitting additional clubs.

The OEMs provide a wide variety of fairway woods and hybrids for fitting purposes. Fairway metals and hybrid clubs are unique in that are used to hit golf balls both on a tee and directly on the turf.

If a golfer wants to be fit for a specific fairway metal or hybrid, I use the same process and principles used for fitting drivers and irons as detailed in the previous two chapters.

If the amateur golfer is being fitted for an entire set of golf clubs, I usually recommend trying the same model of fairway metals and/or hybrids as the driver to which they were fitted. In my experience, amateur golfers usually fit well and like the other fairway metals and hybrids of the same model as their preferred driver. Similar to comparing different models of irons where the 7 iron is usually representative of the entire set of irons, an optimal driver fitting usually relates well to the entire set of fairway metals and hybrids of the same model.

Better players often want to try fairway metals and hybrid models different from their driver model. In my experience, most end up purchasing the same model as their driver.

5 FITTING WEDGES

Wedges are second most used club in a round of golf. As such, it's a very important golf club for hitting greens in regulation and scrambling around the green to save par.

For amateur golfers, I recommend getting the pitching wedge (44-46 degree loft) and gap (G) or approach (A) or utility (U) wedge (48-52 degree loft) with same shafts and fitting specifications (weight and flex) as used in the rest of their iron set.

The sand (S) wedge (54-56 degree loft) and lob (L) wedge (>58 degree loft) are often fitted and purchased separately from the iron set. Why is this? Most of the time, the S and L wedges are swung less than full speed on pitch and chip shots with less centripetal force on the club head, so a flatter (1-2 degrees smaller) lie angle is helpful for making these short golf shots most accurately.

If a golfer wants a slightly flatter lie angle for their wedges, I recommend special ordering the wedges directly from the manufacturer to assure validity of the purchase warranty. Some OEMs will not honor a purchase warranty if the wedges have been bent to adjust the lie angle after purchase.

The key part of the S and L wedge fitting is determining the amount of bounce (mass) needed on the sole of the club. In addition, many wedges are designed with different grinds (customized shaping of the club sole at the leading and trailing edges). Fitting for these club attributes is based on the turf and bunker sand conditions on which these clubs are most frequently used, the golfer's unique angle-of-attack at the golf ball with their club head, and the golfer's feel and personal preference.

The process starts with the golfer interview and discussion of golfer needs and desires for the purchase of new wedges. What wedges do you currently have in your golf set? On the courses where you play golf regularly, are the turf conditions mostly dry and firm or soft and moist? Do you create a divot in the turf when you take a full swing with your wedges? If so, are your divots small, medium, or large? When making pitch and chip shots, do you open or close the club face at set-up before making the shot?

If the golfer uses a specific golf ball to play golf, I use that specific brand and model for the fitting process. I start the fitting process with the golfer's current wedge that they use to make a 40-50 yard shot. I do not put face tape on their wedge, as face tape can significantly decrease the backspin put on the ball with a wedge.

I ask the golfer to step into the golf simulator hitting bay and take 8-10 shots to get warmed up. I record these warm up shots with the simulator program and keep the best 4 or 5 shots as the data representing their optimum performance capability with their current wedge. The key measurements for comparison are distance (carry and total) accuracy (dispersion), and backspin (stopping ability on the green).

I then pick 2-3 S and/or L demo wedge models for the golfer to try hitting in the golf simulator. I will provide key insights on this important choice in the chapter on Selecting Wedges.

If possible, I choose demo wedge shafts similar in flex to those in the iron set of the golfer. I use a relatively new urethane covered golf ball preferred by the golfer. I test wedges on a 40-50 yard pitch shot. The club that gets the most backspin (3,000-6,000 rpm) and stopping power for this short shot is the best quantitatively. Qualitatively, the club should feel good to the golfer.

I then put a piece of fitting tape on the sole of the club, place a golf ball on a fiberglass strike-board, and ask the golfer to take 2-3 full length shots with the wedge. I analyze the strike marks on the club sole tape to see where the ground impact marks are on the sole of the club. If the strike marks are toward the front (target side) of the sole, the golfer's angle of attack is steep. This golfer is a "digger" that usually produces big divots and needs a wedge with a high bounce angle to minimize digging into the turf and optimize impact with the golf ball. The optimum bounce angle on a wedge for a digger is large (>11 degrees). If the sole tape impact mark is in the middle (between the leading and trailing edges of the sole), the golfer should use a wedge with a medium (10-11 degrees) bounce angle to optimize impact with the golf ball. If the sole tape impact marks are toward the back (trailing edge of the sole), this golfer is a "sweeper" and usually takes little or no divot at all. For sweepers, I recommend wedges with a small (<9 degree) bounce angle. For illustrations of this process, see (see https://ping.com/en-us/blogs/proving-grounds/find-your-grind).

If the golfer prefers to manipulate the club face open or closed at address, I may try different wedge grinds that provide relief (forgiveness) at the indicated bounce angle. The testing process of grinds is highly subjective and based qualitatively on golfer feel.

In general, wedge ball striking on hard dry turf conditions or firm (unraked) bunker sand conditions are optimized with low bounce angle wedges, while ball striking on soft moist turf conditions or soft fluffy (raked) sand are optimized with high bounce angle wedges.

6 FITTING PUTTERS

The putter is the MOST important club used in the game of golf. If a scratch (par) golfer hits every green in regulation and 2 putts every green, he/she will strike their putter 36 times in an 18 hole round of golf. That is a total of 36 putting strokes and represents 50% of the shots taken in a round of golf to shoot par (72)! Quantitatively, putting performance is very important for shooting a good golf score.

The preferred putter that optimizes putting performance is a highly personal decision for the golfer. The appropriate shaft length is the most important variable in fitting the amateur golfer with a putter to optimize putting performance.

The process starts with the golfer interview and discussion of golfer needs and desires for the purchase of a new putter. What putter do you currently use? Do you have it with you for comparison to new putters? What do you like about your current putter? When you miss the hole with your current putter, do you miss left or right? Do you prefer a soft or firm feel upon striking the ball when putting? Do you use and value any visual alignment aid markings on the putter? Do you prefer a blade or mallet style putter?

I ask the golfer to roll 5 putts from a distance of 6-8 feet with their current putter on a level straight putting surface. I note the number of putts that drop in the hole and to which side of the hole the misses occur. I observe the golfer's setup, the lie of the putter sole in their setup, how they aim, and the extent of stoke arc when putting.

I take biometric measurements of the golfers height (shoes on) and wrist-to-floor distance of the golfer's non-dominant (lead or target-side) hand. I use the PING putter length chart as a guide for choosing the putter length for new putter testing purposes (see https://ping.com/en-us/fitting/our-process/putter-fitting). For the optimal putter length, it is important that the club head sole lies level and parallel to the ground. If the toe is elevated at setup, I ask the golfer to grip down further (0.5 inch) on the grip toward the club head and get slightly closer to the ball at setup. If the heel is elevated, I ask the golfer to grip further up (0.5 inch) on the grip toward the end of the handle and get slightly further away from the ball at setup. As a visual aid, I use a ground level (shoe) mirror placed on the non-target hole side of the golfer so that he/she can see the sole resting on the ground at set-up. If these minor grip adjustments do result in the sole of the club head resting level and parallel to the ground, I try a longer putter length if the heel is elevated off the ground or a shorter putter length if the toe is elevated off the ground.

From the answers to the interview questions and the information gained watching the golfer hitting putts with their current putter, I choose 3-4 putters for the golfer to try. I will provide key insights on this important choice in the chapter on Selecting Putters.

For each new putter, I ask the golfer to roll 5 putts from a distance of 6-8 feet on a level straight putter surface. I note the number of putts that drop into the hole and to which side of the hole any misses occur.

I then take the top 2 performing putters and ask the golfer to roll 5 additional putts with each club focusing on the quality of the ball strikes, the overall feel of grip and club, and the visual eye appeal of the putter.

I analyze the data from 10 putts with the top two putters. I calculate the number of putts that rolled into the hole and if the missed putts went left or right. For optimal putter performance, I expect the golfer to sink 80-90% of the putts from a 6-8 feet distance.

For the best performing putter, I ask the golfer to set up to make a 6-8 foot putt. I use a ball with a straight line marked on the top side of the ball aimed directly at the hole. I check this straight aim alignment by standing a few feet behind the ball and hold the putter shaft almost vertical in the air at eye level about 12-16 inches in front of me. I align the shaft straight over the line on the ball. If the aiming line on the ball is aligned accurately, the upper portion of the shaft should be in line with the target hole. This process is called "barrel aiming" and is used by many tour pros.

I then place an alignment rod on the ground straight on the target line between the hole and the ball and ask the golfer if the putter head aiming aid markings (if any), the ball aim line, and the alignment rod are visually lined up straight to the hole when they set up to putt the ball. <u>This visual image is most important for getting the ball rolling on the intended target line</u>. When the golfer sees and feels this optimum visual alignment at setup, I ask the golfer to roll 5 more putts from 6-8 feet. I expect the golfer to roll all 5 putts in the hole! When the golfer rolls these putts, the aim line on the ball should roll straight end-over-end without wobbling. When this happens, the golfer has found their optimum putter.

If a golfer wants detailed diagnostic data about their putting stroke, I use the PING putting application for use on a smart phone. PING provides club fitters with a cradle that attaches the phone to the putter shaft. The app uses the phone's gyroscope to provide a wealth of putting stroke diagnostic data (see <u>https://eu.ping.com/en-gb/fitting/iping-2-0-putting-app</u>).

For most amateur golfers, I usually do not make changes to the putter loft. Most new putters have a standard 3 degrees of loft. The loft for optimal putter performance is dependent on the shaft lean at impact during the putting stroke which is sometimes difficult to evaluate accurately with the naked eye. Putter shaft lean at impact can be measured accurately with the PING putter application on a smart phone, but I do not bend new putters to adjust the loft for trial during a fitting. Consideration should also be given to the type of greens on which the golfer usually plays. Golfers that play on "slow" greens with relatively long grass may benefit from a putter with increased loft to initiate the ball rolling well, while golfers that play on relatively "fast" greens with well manicured, short grass may benefit from a putter with decreased loft to minimize back spin and bouncing upon striking the ball. If the putter loft becomes questionable, the golfer can get the loft adjusted anytime after purchase. I recommend that adjustments in putter lie angle be done by the manufacturer, as some OEMs will not honor their purchase warranty if the putter is adjusted by someone else.

Putters should be fitted to optimize making putts at a relatively short (6-8 feet) distance. Making these putts successfully is key to optimizing putter performance and golf scores.

7 FITTING GOLF BALLS

Golfers sometimes want to be "fitted" for a golf ball. Most golf balls on the market are the same size with the exception of Callaway Magna balls. The golfer is simply looking for a recommendation for a ball that "fits" their game.

Titleist is the market leader in golf ball innovation. They recommend a "green to tee" fitting process. Titleist starts the golf ball evaluation process on the green with putting, chipping, and pitch shots, because these are the majority of strokes executed during a round of golf. Iron and driver shots can also be measured and evaluated, but the comparative outcomes and qualitative feel golf balls while putting, chipping, and pitching are most important.

The process starts with the golfer interview and discussion of golfer needs and desires for select a preferred golf ball. What golf ball do you currently use? What do you like most about that ball? Do you prefer the feel and/or sound of a firm or soft golf ball? Do you prefer your pitch shots "check-up" and stop on the green upon landing or do you like them to roll out? What is the maximum price that you would pay for a dozen golf balls?

With answers to these questions, I select three different golf balls for the golfer to try and compare to their current golf ball. I start on the practice putting surface. I ask the golfer to roll 5 putts from a distance of 6-8 feet with their current ball of choice and then the three trial balls selected. I ask the golfer to pay close attention to the qualities of feel and sound upon stroking the ball. When finished, I ask the golfer to rank order his/her preference of these balls. I take the top two ranked balls and move to the hitting bay.

I start this process with the golfer's current wedge that they use to make a 40-50 yard shot. I do not put face tape on their wedge, as face tape can significantly decrease the backspin put on the ball with a wedge.

I ask the golfer to step into the golf simulator hitting bay and take 8-10 shots with their current preferred golf ball at a distance of 40-50 yards to get warmed up. I record these warm up shots with the simulator program and keep the best 4 or 5 shots as the data representing their optimum performance capability with their current wedge. The key measurements for comparison are distance (carry and total) accuracy (dispersion), and backspin (stopping ability).

I then repeat this process with the top two ranked golf balls from the putting trial. The ball with the most accuracy, precision, and backspin is the preferred ball for this golfer.

Additional testing of the top two ranked balls from the cutting trial can be done by hitting full swing iron and driver shots, but the evaluation of ball performance while putting and pitching are most important in my mind.

8 SELECTING IRONS

This chapter provides insights on technologies and innovations that may be useful for selecting a new set of irons. In the chapter on Fitting Irons, I provide details on how these technologies affect golf ball flight and how they are used in fitting process.

What golf clubs should the average amateur golfer try? How do I select the 3 or 4 irons for the golfer to try in the hitting bay? It really depends on the individual's level of talent and skill at playing golf and the amount of money that the golfer is willing to spend for new irons.

New golf irons can be categorized into one of three major categories for most amateur golfers: skilled players clubs, game improvement clubs, and super-game improvement clubs. The differences in these categories are best shown in Table 5.

Within each category, the OEMs have developed sub-categories based on golfer's specific needs. The skilled players irons include "muscle-back (MB) blades" often used by professional golfers on tour, a slightly more forgiving "muscle-cavity back (MC) blade," and a more forgiving "distance players irons" with any combination of increased club head size, decreased (stronger) lofts, increased offset, and increased perimeter weighting when compared to MB blades.

Similar sub-categories have evolved in the game improvement category. Perimeter-weighted cavity back iron heads made of cast steel dominate this category. Distance irons with strong (decreased) lofts have been developed as game improvement clubs. Irons heads made by combining a forged face and cast steel hosel have also evolved as game improvement clubs.

Table 5: Golf Iron Categories

	Skilled Players	Game Improvement	Super-Game Improvement
Handicap	0-9	10-25	>25
Average Score 18 Holes	<85	85-100	>100
Steel	Forged	Forged or Cast	Cast
Club Head Size	Small	Medium	Large
Design	Blade	Cavity Back	Cavity Back and/or Iron-Wood (Hybrid)
Loft	High (Weak)	Medium or Low	Low (Strong)
Center of Gravity (COG)	High (short irons) Low (long irons)	Low	Lowest
Offset	Minimum	Moderate	Maximum
Sole Width	Minimum	Moderate	Maximum
Shaft Weight	Maximum	Moderate	Minimum
Goal	Distance Control Shot Shaping	Foreginess Maximum Distance	Maximum Distance Straight Shots

Super-game improvement clubs include both large cavity back iron heads with wide club head soles and hollow iron-wood (hybrid) clubs designed to help get the ball in the air with ease.

There is another category of clubs for "beginner" golfers. These are sold as a full pre-packaged set of clubs with a golf bag. A packaged set of clubs is a high value purchase, but there is no customized fitting involved. These clubs are primarily for people who are just beginning to play golf and/or unsure of their long-term commitment to playing golf in the future.

For amateur golfers with moderate to low swing speeds (<90 mph), I commonly recommend an iron set containing 5, 6, 7, 8, 9, pitching wedge

(P), and a gap (G) or approach (A) or utility (U) wedge. The loft gapping between irons is usually around 3 degrees for the long irons and increases to 4 degrees for the short irons. In most modern irons for amateurs, the P wedge should be 44-46 degrees of loft, while the G, A, or U wedge should be 48-52 degrees loft. I also recommend a sand (S) wedge (54-56 degree loft) and a lob (L) wedge (>58 degrees). The S and L wedges can be purchased as part of the entire iron set, but many golfers fit and purchase these important clubs separately. Most modern game improvement iron sets do not include a 3 or 4 iron, but they may be available for skilled players clubs.

Mixed or blended sets can also be developed. For example, a golfer may want to use a distance players iron for their short irons (7 thru G, A or U wedge) and a game improvement club for the long irons (6 and 5) which are less forgiving because of less loft.

The steel composition of iron heads influence club selection. Forged iron heads are commonly made of carbon steel that is heated and stamped into the appropriate form and shape. Cast irons are made by pouring molten stainless steel into a specific mold for each iron head. Forged irons are more expensive than cast irons. The carbon steel used to make forged irons is more pliable than the stainless steel in cast irons. As such, forged irons can be physically bent to adjust the lie angle of the club after manufacturing. Bending of cast irons is not recommended, as the stainless steel is very hard and subject to breaking if they are physically bent after manufacturing. Even if cast irons are successfully bent, they sometimes revert back to their original shape.

The most recent technical innovation in irons is the development of hollow body iron heads with or without a polymer filling material. The polymer provides an optimal feel and sound when striking the ball. Face cup head designs involve wrapping the face material around the sole and/or top line of the club. Face cup designs are intended to provide a rebound "trampoline" effect" that maximizes ball speed. Increased perimeter weighting of the iron head (cavity back design) maximizes the moment-of-inertia (MOI) and minimizes twisting of the club head with an off-center face impact with the ball.

Distance irons in the game improvement category have become increasingly popular. Golfers continually want more distance. Increasing iron shot distance by using a clubs with strong (decreased) loft angles comes with a trade-off effect of decreased ball spin and stopping power on the greens. In essence, the loft on a game improvement distance PW may be similar to the loft on a non-distance designed 9 iron. This approach may create large loft gaps between some of the short scoring irons. When considering the purchase of new game improvement irons, the golfer needs to decide whether distance or stopping power is most important for their game improvement. In my opinion, the short scoring irons lofts should be gapped to maximize stopping power and reach greens in regulation.

Some OEMs have increased the number and size of grooves on the face of some iron models. In reality, the main purpose of grooves on irons is to dispose of moisture, grass, and debris that decrease friction between the golf ball and the club face at impact. The iron face grooves essentially function like the tread grooves on an automobile snow tire that disperse the snow and moisture and maximize contact of the tire rubber with the pavement. Contrary to popular belief, the grooves contribute to less than 10% of the resulting spin on the golf ball. Experimentally, irons with no grooves create maximum friction and can spin a golf ball very well. Auto drag racers use tires without tread grooves (slicks) to maximize contact friction with the pavement. Maximum speed and friction between the face of the iron and a golf ball with a soft cover material is what imparts the vast majority of spin on the golf ball.

As for specific brands and models, all of the OEMs make excellent high quality golf equipment. The dollar share market leaders for irons sold to amateur golfers are Callaway, TaylorMade, and PING. Historically, Titleist and Mizuno are known for making high quality players clubs. Titleist irons are played by many tour pros, and they have recently developed models in the super-game improvement category. Mizuno is known for using exceptional high quality materials in their irons. Golfers that use Mizuno irons are the most brand loyal customers that I have met. Cobra, Cleveland, Srixon, XXIO, and PXG also make high quality irons with models in all categories. Wilson is a brand with historical prestige and offers iron models in all categories. Tour Edge is a value brand and a leader in market volume share. You can't go wrong with clubs from any of this OEM brands.

My approach to iron selection is brand agnostic. The decision on which irons the golfer buys is often determined by brand loyalty, demo trial performance, and the price point at which the golfer is willing to buy. The visual appearance of the iron is important for many golfers. A small iron club head with a thin top line is preferred by many better players. My job as a professional golf club fitter is to help amateur golfers understand the available technologies and options available, put the iron most likely to perform well in the golfer's hands, and optimize their demo trial performance. The golfer's job is to try the clubs and be delighted with their choice and the improved performance in their golf game.

9 SELECTING DRIVERS

This chapter provides insights on technologies and innovations that may be useful for selection of a driver. In the chapter on Fitting Drivers, I provide details on how these technologies affect golf ball flight, diagnostic data, and how they are used in fitting process.

The driver is the second most important club for fitting purposes behind the putter. It is the most difficult club in the golf bag to hit, because it has the least amount of loft. Everyone wants to hit the ball far off of the tee box. Distance is a key priority, but how one gets maximum distance depends on how fast they can swing the club and where they make contact with the ball on the face of the club. Shot distance is maximized with center hits on the driver club face. Actually the ideal place on the driver club face for impact to maximize distance is slightly (0.25 inch) above the geometric center of the club face.

Innovation in driver technology has been extensive. Almost all modern drivers are large (460 cc maximum) and utilize hollow body designs made of a combination of metal (titanium) and carbon materials. The carbon components are relatively light and allow key placement of the metal components within the club head to maximize MOI for forgiveness on off-center hits and position the COG in specific areas of the club to influence ball flight. PING drivers are known for producing drivers with maximum MOI that are very forgiving.

Club manufacturers produce driver models with either fixed or adjustable loft, face angle, COG, and lie angle. Adjustable hosel shaft adapters and movable weights on the driver club head are remarkable innovations that allow the golfer to make adjustments on their driver as needed. In reality, many golfers simply don't feel comfortable making these adjustments. In addition, these add-on technologies increase the cost of the driver. Drivers with a fixed loft, face angle, COG, and lie angle will cost less than those with adjustability.

The hosel shaft adapter can vary the loft, face angle, and lie angle of the club. The Titleist SureFit® hosel shaft adapter provides 16 different settings for adjusting these variables. This is adjusted by using a hand-held torque wrench to unloosen the hosel screw that attaches the driver head to the shaft to change the settings. Each OEM makes a unique hosel shaft adapter specifically designed for their drivers and provides detailed charts on the intended effects that these adapter adjustments will effect.

TaylorMade and Callaway have led innovation in driver face design. They developed their Twist Face technology in 2018 to provide forgiveness on high-toe and low-heel face impacts with the ball. These are the most common mishits made by amateur golfers with their drivers. With Twist Face drivers, the face of the driver is slightly twisted to increase the loft and open the face angle in the high-toe area and decrease the loft and close the face angle in the low-heel area of the face. These alterations help minimize high-toe hit hooks and low-heel hit slices. TaylorMade is also the first OEM to use multiple layers of carbon material to construct the entire club face in their Stealth™ driver model. Callaway has also led in development of driver face design using artificial intelligence (AI) to screen prototypes of variable-face-thickness to optimize backspin and forgiveness with off-center ball impact.

Cobra was the first to use CNC (computer numerical controlled) milled faces on their drivers. This process produces drivers with high precision and consistency in driver face production. In contrast, most other titanium driver faces are forged or cast and hand ground and polished before product release. As such, the Cobra CNC driver that a golfer buys off the rack in a retail store is most similar to the demo club that they hit in the fitting bay.

Regardless of the impressive OEM marketing claims made about the reactivity of their driver club faces, the manufacture and release specifications of all golf clubs is regulated by the United States Golf Association (USGA) and Royal and Ancient (R&A) Golf Club of Scotland. All drivers are released into the market based on characteristic time (CT) measurements. The CT is the time that a standardized steel metal ball remains in contact with the face of a driver when applied at a standardized force delivered by a testing device with a steel ball on a pendulum. All legal drivers released for marketing must have a CT between 221-257 milliseconds. Those drivers with CTs in the high end of this range have the most spring-board effect on the ball resulting in higher ball speeds and shot distance. As such, there is some variability in the spring-board effects of drivers on the retail shelf. My guess is that drivers with the highest CTs are most likely targeted for use by professional golfers and as retail demo clubs, and the rest (lowest CTs) are sold to consumer amateur golfers. As such, a demo driver that a golfer hits in the fitting bay may be "hotter" (high CT with maximal spring-board effect) in testing than the club that they may purchase off of the retail store display rack. I always recommend that a golfer test and purchase a driver that they have hit in the fitting bay. This can be done effectively by putting a piece of face tape on the new driver from the retail display rack and hitting it in the fitting bay.

Another big innovation in drivers is the entry of the ultra-light driver category with 30-40 gram weight class shafts. XXIO is a Japanese company that designed golf clubs for small people with moderate to low swing speeds. Cleveland Golf launched the XXIO brand in the United States and targeted senior golfers. XXIO offers a premium priced driver that has had remarkable success in the US market. Seniors simply love these clubs. Callaway and Titleist were fast-followers launching ultra-light models for US consumers.

10 SELECTING FAIRWAY METALS & HYBRIDS

For the amateur golfer looking for an entire set of clubs, I usually recommend selection of the same model of fairway metals and hybrids as the driver to which they were fitted. In my experience, amateur golfers usually fit well and like the other fairway metals and hybrids of the same model as their preferred driver. Similar to comparing different models of irons where the 7 iron is usually representative of the entire set of irons, an optimal driver fitting usually relates well to the entire set of fairway metals and hybrids of the same model.

The shafts of the fairway metals chosen are usually 10 grams heavier than the weight of the driver shaft, while the shafts of the hybrids are usually 20 grams heavier than the weight of the driver shaft.

11 SELECTING WEDGES

This chapter provides insights on technologies and innovations that may be useful for selection of wedges. In the chapter on Fitting Wedges, I provide details on how these technologies affect golf ball back spin, stopping power on the greens, and how they are used in fitting process.

For amateur golfers buying modern golf clubs, I recommend selecting a pitching wedge (44-46 degree loft) and gap (G), approach (A) or utility (U) wedge (48-52 degree loft) with the same shafts and fitting specifications (weight and flex) as used in the rest of their iron set.

The sand (S) wedge (54-56 degree loft) and lob (L) wedge (>58 degree loft) are often fitted and purchased separately from the iron set. Why is this? Most of the time, the S and L wedges are swung less than full speed on pitch and chip shots with less centripetal force on the club head, so a flatter (1-2 degrees smaller) lie angle is helpful for making these short golf shots most accurately.

The key part of the S and L wedge selection is determining the amount of bounce (mass) on the sole of the club needed. In addition, many wedges are designed with different grinds (custom shaping of the club sole at the leading and trailing edges). Fitting for these club attributes is based on the turf and bunker sand conditions on which these clubs are most frequently used, the golfer's unique angle-of-attack at the golf ball with the club head, and the golfer's feel and personal preference.

In general, wedge ball striking on hard dry turf conditions or firm (unraked) bunker sand conditions are optimized with low bounce angle wedges, while ball striking on soft moist turf conditions or soft fluffy (raked) bunker sand are optimized with high bounce angle wedges.

Titleist dominates the wedge market for better players with their

BV (Bob Vokey) wedges. Better players love to try a few of at least six different grind models, most custom designed for PGA Tour players. Wedge selection is aided by an on-line fitting tool that helps narrow down the numerous options available by answering several questions about their wedge play (see https://www.vokey.com/tools/wedge-selector-tool.aspx).

Cleveland Golf offers a wide selection of wedges for amateur golfers including models designed for better players (RTX), game improvement (CBX), and super-game improvement (Smart Sole). Their iconic V-sole design is simple, versatile, and available in 3 different grinds.

The biggest technical innovation in S and L wedges has been the development of small micro-ridges between the face grooves by Roger Cleveland at Callaway. The additional micro-ridges between the large grooves maximize friction and "bite" to increase spin and stopping power of the ball. Callaway also developed an offset "groove-in-groove" technology which has small milled micro-grooves on a 20 degree angle (running from low on the toe to high on the heel of the club). These additional grooves are designed to disperse moisture and debris at impact and enhance spin on open-faced shots.

"Raw" is an innovation popularized by TaylorMade that is designed to increase friction and back spin. The face of raw wedges are not plated, i.e., coated with protectant finish. It is claimed that this allows increased contact of the ball with the edges of the face grooves. As the club face is not coated and unprotected, the face rusts over time with exposure to moisture and air and produces a visibly rough (red-brown) club face that increases friction and ball spin.

Several OEMs have developed enlarged wedge heads by extending the face on top of the toe region. This raises the COG of the club and produces a low trajectory shot for more control. Some models have grooves that extend across the entire face of the club.

For clarity, the primary function of the face grooves on any iron is to disperse moisture, grass, and debris that decrease friction and spin. PING produces wedges with superior performance in wet conditions.

Almost all of the OEMs mill (grind) at least some of the wedge club face to create a rough surface that creates friction and increases ball backspin.

Also worth mentioning, Edison wedges are an excellent choice for amateur golfers available on-line, direct-to-consumers. Edison designer,

Terry Koehler, has created a simple V-sole design that is versatile and works for many swing types and turf and sand conditions played. Edison wedge's high COG produces shots with a low trajectory for control and high ball backspin for stopping power on the green.

Most of the wedges available in retail outlets have steel shafts, and they vary in shaft flex and weight. Common wedge flex designations and their corresponding weights are presented in Table 6.

TABLE 6: Wedge Shaft Flex and Weights

Shaft Flex	Weight (g)
Wedge (W)	122
Wedge Plus (W+)	128
R200/R300/R400	125/127/129
S200/S300/S400	129/130/132
X100/X200/X300/X400	130/130/132/134

Ultimately, the selection of wedges is a highly personal decision based on the golfer's swing dynamics and turf and sand conditions played most often. Better players often have two sets of wedges: one for playing firm tight turf and bunker conditions and another for playing soft turf and fluffy sand bunkers.

12 SELECTING PUTTERS

This chapter provides insights on technologies and innovations that may be useful for selection of a putter. In the chapter on Fitting Putters, I provide details on how these technologies affect golf ball starting direction and how they are used in fitting process.

The putter is the MOST important club used in the game of golf. Putting is most important, because approximately 40-50% of the strokes in an 18 hole round of golf are executed with the putter.

Putting a golf ball is simple and requires the least physical skill to perform successfully when compared to all of the other golf clubs and the swings needed to make successful golf shots. The putter used by a golfer is a highly personal choice that they must feel comfortable and confident using.

The two main putter head designs are blades and mallets. In general, blade putter heads are smaller, lighter in weight, and thinner than mallets. Blades are generally thought to work well for golfers with moderate to large swing arcs, while mallets work best for golfers with a minimal swing arc. Mallet heads are larger and heavier in weight than blades and have their mass distributed throughout the club head which increases perimeter weighting and MOI to minimize twisting of the face with off-center face contact with the golf ball. As such, mallet putter heads are more forgiving when compared to blades. There are putter heads (mid-mallets) available that are intermediate in size and weight compared to most blades and mallets.

The key design feature that influences putter face speed of rotation during a swing is where the shaft is aligned or attaches to the putter head. If the shaft is aligned or attaches near the heel of the putter, the putter toe and center of the face will rotate faster than the heel during a stroke. Heel-shaft alignment is often used in blade putters and is the rationale for golfers using blade putters optimally with a moderate to large swing arc.

If you hold a putter with heel-shaft alignment horizontally resting the shaft on your two index fingers held about 18 inches apart, the toe of the putter head will hang down from the horizontal plane and is referred to as "toe-hang". Toe-hang of 0-20 degrees is minimal, 20-60 degrees is moderate, while >60 degrees is marked. Heel-shaft aligned putters usually have moderate to marked toe-hang. If there is no tow-hang, the putter is referred to as being "face-balanced".

If the shaft is aligned or attaches near the center of the club head, the center of the face will rotate relatively slowly compared to the heel and toe during the stroke. Center-shaft alignment is often used in mallet putters and is the rationale for golfers using mallet putters optimally with a minimal swing arc. Center-shaft aligned putters usually have minimal toe-hang or are face-balanced.

In my opinion, extent of toe-hang only indicates where the club shaft aligns or attaches into the putter head. No golfer ever holds their putter horizontally to putt, so a putter being face-balanced when held horizontal is of little, if any, relevance to the putting stroke.

In contrast, if you insert a golf tee in the end of the putter grip, gently grab that tee, hold the putter vertical at the angle of address, balance the putter shaft with the index finger of your other hand held just below the grip, and swing the putter gently in a putting stroke motion at your normal setup angle, you will be able to see the effects of club design on torque (twisting or rotation) during a putting stroke. I prefer putters where the face remains square to the target (no rotation) during the stroke. This is referred to as being "lie angle balanced". Center shafted mallet putters are sometimes lie-angle balanced. Specifically designed lie angle balanced putters are available commercially from L.A.B. Golf online (see https://labgolf.com/).

It is controversial among experts on which shaft alignment (heel or center) best optimizes missed putts. The major OEM recommendations for a putter design that helps correct a push (miss right for right handed golfer) or pull (miss left for a right handed golfer) differ. In a heel-shaft aligned putter, the face center and toe move at a faster rate than the heel when the shaft is rotated with a standard force. In contrast, in a center-shaft aligned putter, the center of the face will rotate relatively slowly compared to the heel and toe when the shaft is rotated at the same force. The difference is that it takes more force to rotate a heel-shaft aligned putter shaft to a standardized rate when compared to a center-shaft aligned putter shaft. The reality is that a golfer's outcome (left or right) with these putter designs is "player and swing dependent". As such, if a golfer is trying to correct a common miss left or right, I recommend that a golfer try both heel and center shaft alignment designs to see what works best for them. In reality, it's the outcome (holed putts) that matters most.

The look and appearance of a putter is very important to instill confidence for putting. If a golfer prefers blades, I select blades for them to try. The same goes for mallets. Mid-mallets are another option. Many putters have visual alignment aids (painted lines or dots) that may help the golfer align the face of the putter square with their ball and the target start line. I recommend putters with visual alignment aids for aiming purposes. Surprisingly, many amateur golfers do not aim when setting up to stroke a putt!

PING designs their putters based on physical appearance and visual appeal to aid alignment and aim to get the golf ball started on the intended target line. PING designs their putters in four basic archetypes. Archetype 1 is for golfers that primarily utilize the top rail of the putter head for visual alignment and aiming. Archetype 2 is for golfers that use visual alignment features that "frame the ball". Archetype 3 is for golfers that use prominent long alignment features, while archetype 4 is for golfers that use an alignment feature that runs all the way to the ball (see https://ping.com/en-us/blogs/proving-grounds/putter-alignment). The physical appearance and visual appeal of the putter are very important for alignment and aiming the putter head.

SeeMore putters have a unique RifleScope technology (red dot on the top of the heel of the putter head) that is used to standardize setup. By positioning the shaft to visually cover and eliminate the red dot from the view of the golfer, a golfer can standardize their setup posture and hopefully the precision of their putting stroke.

The feel of a putter when striking the ball is a highly personal preference for selection of a putter. A firm feel and sound is obtained with milled or smooth metal face putter, while a soft feel is obtained from putters with a face insert.

Odyssey makes a Microhinge face insert with many small micro-hinges across the putter face that flex and push the golf ball forward at impact to enhance top spin and minimize backspin. TaylorMade developed the Pure Roll face technology consisting of horizontal aluminum slats angled at 45 degrees to the vertical face of the putter and provides a similar flex effect on impact with the golf ball that enhances top spin and forward roll. Odyssey also developed the historically popular soft White Hot face insert. PING Sigma 2 putter face inserts are very soft for golfers that prefer soft feel when putting.

Like all the other clubs in the golf bag, the optimal putter shaft for a golfer is determined primarily by qualitative feel. Most putter shafts are steel, but Odyssey offers their Stroke Lab putter shaft that is light weight (75 gram) and made of a combination of graphite in the grip end and steel attaching to the putter head. They redistribute 50 grams of weight from the center of the shaft by putting 10 grams of weight in the putter head and 40 grams of weight in the grip end of the shaft. Independent testing shows improved putting performance with this multi-material shaft when compared to traditional steel shafts (https://mygolfspy.com/odyssey-stroke-lab-putters-vs-non-stroke-lab-putters/). UST-Mamiya produces a similar multi-material putter shaft (ALL-IN).

PING offers a unique putter grip that allows easy manual adjustment of the overall club length by twisting a screw in the end of the grip. They also offer a putter head (Fetch) with a perfectly sized hole in the club head that allows easy pick-up and retrieval of a golf ball even when in the hole. This is helpful for golfers that have physical limitations that inhibit their ability to bend down to pick up their golf ball.

13 SELECTING SHAFTS

All modern driver shafts are made of graphite. Iron shafts are made of steel or graphite depending on the flex (weight) required, but there is a popular composite steel-graphite shaft (Aerotech SteelFiber) available for irons. Most putter shafts are made of steel, but there are innovative light-weight combination steel-graphite (Odyssey Stroke Lab, UST ALL-IN) putter shafts available.

The most important factors in choosing a golf shaft is the shaft weight and the qualitative feel to the golfer. The weight of shafts are commonly referred to as a "weight class" range, because the absolute weight of each shaft will vary slightly when trimmed to the needed length for each club in the set. In general, the higher the weight of the shaft, the less flexible the shaft will be. Steel shafts range in weight between 80-130 grams, while graphite shafts range in weight 30-80 grams.

Changing the shaft weight and/or flex can alter shot trajectory. If a golfer's main missed shot pattern is a hook, a heavier and/or stiffer flex shaft may help minimize the hook. Conversely, if a golfer's main miss is a slice, a lighter and/or more flexible shaft may help minimize the slice.

The flex designation of shafts is often over-interpreted. There is no standardized method for OEMs to measure shaft flex. As such, OEMs use different methods to measure shaft flex, so comparison of the flex of one brand of shaft to another is questionable. In general, PING shafts are commonly thought among club fitters to be softer and more flexible than other OEM shafts of an equivalent flex designation.

In my experience, men simply do not like the senior flex designation. Most men are insulted if I suggest they try a senior flex shaft.

PING designates their senior flex shafts as soft regular (SR). This designation is much more acceptable psychologically to older men. No one but you will know you may be hitting a senior flex shaft. Has anyone ever grabbed your club on the golf course and asked, "What flex is your shaft?" I doubt it. In addition, no one else really cares.

Much has been written about kick (flex or bend) points and the tip stiffness/softness of golf shafts and how these variables can may help one predict performance and choose the best golf shaft. My advanced golf club fitter training from Callaway taught me some important information. In theory, a high shaft kick point is associated with a stiff tip and a low ball launch angle, while a low kick point is associated with soft tip and a high ball launch angle. The kick points of golf shafts are located at a position approximately 45% of the distance from the tip of the shaft. The difference in the highest and lowest kick points in a graphite or steel golf shaft is about 1.5 inches. Being this close together, the shaft bend points have little effect on golf ball trajectory when swung at the moderate to low swing speeds of most amateur golfers, but they have a significant effect on swing feel to the golfer.

Similarly, torque (the angular rotation in degrees about the shaft's longitudinal axis when a load is applied) has little to no effect on pre-impact face angle but major effects on post-impact feel and vibration. For the record, low torque shafts have 2-3 degrees of rotation, standard or mid-torque shafts have 4-6 degrees of rotation, while high torque shafts have more than 6 degrees of rotation. I've never fitted a golf club based on the torque of the shaft.

For the record, the shafts of the fairway metals chosen are usually 10 grams heavier than the weight of the driver shaft, while the shafts of the hybrids are usually 20 grams heavier than the weight of the driver shaft.

If a golfer swings their driver club head >100 mph, they may benefit from trying a high-tech after-market shaft. In my opinion, it's only at very high swing speeds that a golfer may feel potential differences and see benefits from these advanced shaft technologies.

Most amateur golfers have driver club head speeds <100 mph. Before an amateur golfer purchases an expensive after-market shaft, they should read this quote by Mr. Frank Thomas, Technical Director of the United States Golf Association (USGA) for 26 years and Golf Digest Chief Technical Advisor. Mr. Thomas invented the graphite golf shaft. He said, "During impact, the shaft is unnecessary. Its only use is to get the club into the proper position, traveling on the right path and at the required speed just before impact. Remember that impact, when the club and the ball are actually in contact, only lasts for approximately 450 millionths of a second. When the shaft decides to react to a mis-hit, the ball is long gone, so it plays no part in reducing an error, contrary to what is sometimes believed."

By analogy, an expensive high-performance Ferrari automobile may be appropriate if you routinely drive on the Autobahn in Germany with no speed limit, but a high-value, mid-size Chevrolet is just fine for routine travel to and from the local grocery store in the United States.

The reality is that driver and iron shaft performance is highly "player and swing dependent," and the best shaft fit for a golfer is primarily based on the qualitative feel to the golfer. This is particularly true for amateur golfers with moderate to low swing speeds. The golf shafts offered by the OEMs as standard equipment are of excellent quality and sufficient for optimally fitting almost all amateur golfers.

14 SELECTING GRIPS

The selection of golf club grips is a personal preference decision primarily determined by feel to the golfer. Grips come in standard, midsize, jumbo, ladies, and extra-small (junior or kids) sizes. Most of the demo clubs used in the fitting process for drivers, irons, fairway metals, and wedges have standard sized rubber grips.

The size of a grip can be increased by putting extra layers of grip tape on the butt of the shaft under the grip. The addition of 4 layers of tape is sufficient to increase a grip one full size. For example, a regular size grip with an additional 4 layers of tape underneath produces the same in outer diameter as a midsize grip. Some golfers place additional layers of tape under the lower half of the grip only to reduce tension and increase power of the lower hand on the grip. Some grip manufacturers make grips with the lower half of the grip already enlarged in diameter, e.g., Golf Pride® MCC Plus4 and Lamkin Plus-Reduced Taper.

The most important factor in choosing grips is the weight of the grip. Standard rubber golf grips weigh approximately 50 grams. Rubber is a dense material and can add significant weight to a club with addition of a rubber mid-size or jumbo grip. Mid-size rubber grips can weigh up to 65 grams. Addition of significant weight to the grip end of the club can decrease swingweight, feel for the club head, and shot performance. If you prefer mid-size or jumbo grips, choose a model made of relatively light weight material. Synthetic polymer grip materials are lighter and a better option when choosing large (mid-size or jumbo) grip sizes. Mid-size Winn Dri-Tac grips are equivalent in weight to standard rubber grips. Adding layers of tape also increases club weight. Each full layer of tape adds 2 grams of weight to the club.

Some OEMs (PING, Cobra) offer new clubs with Arrcos Caddie Smart Grip sensors pre-installed with purchase of new irons. These smart clubs allow digital recording of comprehensive shot data from clubs with the sensor chip installed in the grip for a limited trial period. A subscription to the digital recording service can be purchased separately at any time after the trial period.

Most modern putters have large over-sized grips. Some are available with variable sized weights that screw into the end of the putter grip. This counter balancing or "back weighting" effectively reduces swingweight and makes the putter head feel relatively light.

Putter grips come are offered in two basic shapes: straight and contoured. The contoured "pistol" grip is popular. Research by PING has shown that contoured pistol grips produce a statistically significant closed face angle and higher lie angle (toe up) at impact that may result in pulled putts (miss left for right handed golfer) when compared to straight putter grips (see https://ping.com/en-us/blogs/proving-grounds/pistol-grips). As such, a pistol grip may help right handed golfers that consistently push their putts to the right of the hole.

15 SELECTING GOLF BALLS

The golf ball is the only piece of golf equipment that is used on every shot! As such, selection of golf balls is important. Many amateur golfers do not put much thought into the purchase of golf balls, and their choice is highly influenced by cost. Before purchasing golf balls, the golfer needs to determine what qualities they desire most from a ball.

Most amateur golfers want maximum distance from a golf ball. The reality is that most of the high-quality "tour" golf balls on the market fly approximately the same distance when hit with the standardized club by a mechanized golf robot. The absolute differences are minimal (5-10 yards).

Better golfers desire golf balls that they can spin and control well on approach shots. Stopping power on the green is affected primarily by back spin. As such, a soft urethane cover is ideal for generating back spin and used on almost all high-quality tour golf balls. Value (low cost) golf balls commonly have a hard ionomer polymer cover (Surylin®) and do not spin as much as urethane covered balls.

The feel of the ball to the golfer is also an important quality. Many golfers prefer a soft feel upon striking the ball. The feel of the golf ball is primarily determined by the overall hardness of the ball. The hardness of golf balls is determined by measuring "compression". The harder the ball, the more resistant the ball is to physical deformation when compressed in a vice-like device. It takes more force to compress a hard golf ball than a soft one. Technically, compression is measured by applying force to a golf ball to squeeze and deform the ball a standardized distance, e.g., 0.1 inch. This force is converted mathematically to a compression value. Golf balls with compression values >90 are considered high compression or hard, values 70-90 are medium compression, and values <70 are considered low compression or soft.

The overall compression value for a golf ball is determined by the materials and number of layers that make up the core of the ball. A golf ball with a core consisting of multiple layers of rubber and plastic is more resistant to physical compression and feels harder than a ball with fewer layers. Adding layers to the golf ball core increases the cost of manufacturing and the price of the golf ball. Most high-quality tour golf balls consist of 3 or 4 layers (pieces). TaylorMade produces some 5 piece balls (TP5 and TP5x), and Honma produces a 6 piece ball (Future XX).

The controversial issue with compression is that there is no standard method used for measurement within the industry. As such, compression values generated by one OEM may not be meaningfully comparable to values provided by another OEM.

The best and most recent comparisons of golf ball compression are conducted and published on www.myGolfSpy.com (see https://mygolfspy.com/golf-ball-compression-guide/). These independent research studies are conducted scientifically and use one method for measuring compression of almost all golf balls on the market. The key finding from these studies is that hard, high compression golf balls fly further and spin more than soft, low compression balls.

Striking a golf ball with a golf club will deform and compress the ball even at relatively low club head speeds. Golfers should be most concerned about compressing a golf ball too much when they strike it. For maximum performance (distance and stopping power), the best ball for a golfer is the one with the highest compression and acceptable feel to the golfer. For maximum distance, I recommend that an amateur golfer select and use a golf ball with a compression value equal to or higher than their driver club head speed (mph).

A golfer may also select a golf ball for a specific shot flight trajectory. Shot trajectory (low, medium, high) can be varied directly by the amount of backspin and the dimple pattern on the ball cover. A golf ball model name that includes an X usually indicates a ball with a high compression value and a high shot trajectory associated with high backspin. As an example, the Titleist high-quality tour golf balls ProV1x, ProV1, and AVX (Alternative to V and X) have high, medium and low shot trajectories, respectively. Similar nomenclature is used for other high-quality golf ball brand models.

16 SELECTING GOLF INSTRUCTORS

Now that you understand the golf club fitting process and have selected your new clubs, it's time to play golf! In my opinion, new well-fitted golf equipment can improve your golf scores in the range of 10-15%. If you want additional improvement in your golf game, I recommend you take golf lessons from a certified PGA Professional golf instructor.

How do you select a good golf instructor? It depends on what you want to improve in your golf game. To improve your golf game, you need to learn several different types of golf shots including putting, chipping, pitching, bunker shots, full shots with irons, and full shots with the driver. If you sign up for lessons, it's most cost-effective to pre-purchase several lessons as a bundle. It may take several lessons before the golfer is successful implementing any recommended setup and swing changes and seeing positive results on the golf course in a round of golf.

I have taken golf lessons from several PGA certified professional golfers during my lifetime. This instruction has occurred at golf course practice ranges, at indoor facilities with a golf simulator, and on the golf course in a real-time playing lesson.

In my experience, the best golf instructors were the ones that carefully evaluated their students' biometrics, physical capability, and natural swing tendencies and made recommendations for improvement based on their existing skills, swing dynamics, and strengths as the golfer. In contrast, my least helpful lessons were ones trying to make big changes in my swing to make it look like that of a popular tour pro. Everyone's golf swing is unique. Changing it a lot is really difficult and takes a long time.

I'm admire the instructional approach of Mr. Mike Adams from Fiddler's Elbow Country Club in Bedminster, NJ. Mr. Adams BioSwingDynamics program leverages the natural grip and swing dynamics of the golfer (see https://www.golfdigest.com/story/which-backswing-is-for-you-match-your-body-and-grip and https://golf.com/instruction/which-backswing-works-best-for-you/).

I also subscribe to Mr. Mike Malaska's golf instruction website (https://www.malaskagolf.com/). Mr. Malaska was the PGA National Teacher of the year in 2011, and he has a gift for communicating in simple terms. The Malaska Golf website has an excellent library of videos for golf instruction.

Over time, my golf swing and game have evolved to co-exist with my aging knees and back. I played golf with low back and hip pain for several years until I found the "stack-and-tilt" golf swing. I then pursued a stack-and-tilt certified PGA instructor to help me optimize this unique golf swing. Thankfully, I now play golf relatively pain-free at the seasoned age of 67.

17 CARE & MAINTENANCE

Fitted golf clubs are expensive, so you should take care of them to maximize their longevity. Here are some tips to do this.

Use a combo brush with both nylon and wire bristles to clean your clubs of debris. Use the nylon bristles first. They do not damage the milling on some club face surfaces. If the nylon bristles don't do the job, use the wire bristles but use them gently.

Wash golf grips at least once a month with warm soapy water. You'll be surprised how dirty your grips get and how this improves your golf grip and performance. Consider getting new grips every year.

Don't store golf clubs in hot dry environments for long periods of time. Hot and dry temperatures dry out and deteriorate golf club grips quickly. This is particularly a problem with golf club storage in cars and garages in Arizona!

Consider replacing S and L wedges every year. Depending on how much you play, wedges start to wear out after about 70-80 rounds.

Consider purchasing new irons every 5-7 years to leverage new technology. Consider purchasing a new driver at least every 5 years.

You can use powdered foot spray on your driver face to face map your ball impact pattern during practice sessions without damaging it. A light coating of foot powder spray on the face of the driver allows one to see clearly where you are hitting the ball on the face. When finished, the remaining powder can be wiped off easily with a golf towel without damaging the club face of the driver.

If you lose a golf club from a set that is no longer being manufactured, you can find individual clubs on https://www.golfclubfinder.com/.

18 TESTIMONIALS

"I wanted to take the time to provide feedback on my experience today with Kurt. I have never purchased a driver brand new retail, but decided it was time for my 40th birthday present to myself. I was always reserved about taking the time to try different drivers and make changes to really find the right fit.

Kurt was so friendly and patient with me while I asked multiple questions, and we tried lots of different drivers. Once we had narrowed down the driver that would work for me, I asked about less expensive types in the same line. This did not deter Kurt for a second, and he quickly went to older TaylorMade models for me to try. Once we had determined that the M5 was the right one for me, I thought it was over. Kurt assured me that we were not done and that it was time to maximize the features of the new M5 driver to optimize my result. After some quick changes and confirmation from the numbers, we were ready to go.

Just as we were about to leave the hitting bay, another sales associate brought a couple to Kurt for him to assist. Despite my sale essentially being complete, Kurt did not pass me off, but rather stayed and completed my special order with TaylorMade. He looked at every detail down to the grip and made special order instructions for the specific grip I wanted (that was not in the TaylorMade ordering system).

I can't say thank you enough for the fitting experience and service that Kurt provided me. I have always been a PGA Tour Superstore customer over the others, and this experience confirmed for me the reasons why."

Bryan P.
March 2019

"I was a customer at your North Scottsdale store today. I was in search of a putter and was convinced after self-diagnosis I was an arching putter in need of a Scotty Cameron. After hitting a few balls with a few putters, I saw very little improvement in comparison to my current putter.

I was then approached by Kurt Weingand and asked if I needed assistance. I explained my self-diagnosis and current dilemma. He patiently walked me through a few putters and provided feedback. Kurt took the time to analyze my swing and stance. We learned I was a front to back putter with little to no arch.

I am now the proud owner of a Bettinardi Ss28 center shaft putter. It may seem as though it's all in a day's work but little did Kurt know my journey through this wonderful game of golf. I have had multiple poor fittings that led to bad purchases. You can say I am not your stereotypical golfer. When I enter a golf store I struggle to get assistance or people willing to slow down to explain the difference in products. Being a 280 pound ex-powerlifter you don't get many people that will take the time to help you out.

It was a true pleasure working with Kurt and I am grateful for his professionalism and wiliness to educate a customer. As a person that manages 3000 employees over 6 states I truly understand the value of good employees that are willing to go the extra mile. You definitely have a repeat customer with me."

Johnathan L.
September 2018

"I shop at this PGA Superstore often but an experience I had yesterday was exceptional. I had a friend visiting from out of state so I took him to this store to maybe buy a new driver and 3 wood.

Your store representative, Kurt Weingand, could not have been more helpful and patient than he was. Having no idea if there would be a sale or not, he simply was so professional in how he handled my guest. Roger had no choice but to buy his new equipment right then and there.

It's nice to share a good story once in a while."

Carl M.
April 2020

"I was just in the Mayo Blvd store and was fitted for a set of clubs with Kurt. He was very helpful and knowledgeable in getting me the best clubs to work for me. I own a few businesses and it was nice to see that an employee took pride and ownership to give 5 star service to his customer. A rare find these days. He is an asset to your company. Just wanted to share with you."

Rick K
October 2019

"I just wanted to reach out and let you know how much my wife and I really appreciated Kurt helping us choose the right club. He went into great detail and time on showing us the different wedges to buy, and I appreciated his ability to communicate the differences. Very nice employee to talk with. He was able to get down to our bogey level of knowledge and give us so much more. I just thought you should know how much we appreciated his time."

Joe T.
October 2018

ABOUT THE AUTHOR

Kurt Weingand, Ph.D., D.V.M., is a retired veterinarian, biomedical scientist, and college professor that worked 20 years in healthcare product development for The Procter & Gamble Company and 3 years in the College of Veterinary Medicine at Midwestern University. Upon retirement from a career in life sciences, Dr. Weingand pursued his passion and began working in the golf industry. Kurt became a professional golf club fitter in the golf specialty retail channel working at the PGA Tour Superstore, Golf Galaxy, and the Golf Exchange in Phoenix, AZ and Cincinnati, OH. Dr. Weingand is currently a "snowbird" that spends his time playing golf in Phoenix during the winter and spring and works part-time as a Clubhouse Coordinator at Sharon Woods Golf Course in Cincinnati, OH during the summer and fall.

Made in the USA
Columbia, SC
19 January 2023